Celtic Mandala Coloring Book

Relax with this Calming, Stress Managment, Celtic Mandala Coloring Book for Adults

Grahame David Garlick

www.southshorepublications.com

Copyright © 2015 SouthShore Publications

ISBN-13: 978-1519100603

ISBN-10: 1519100604

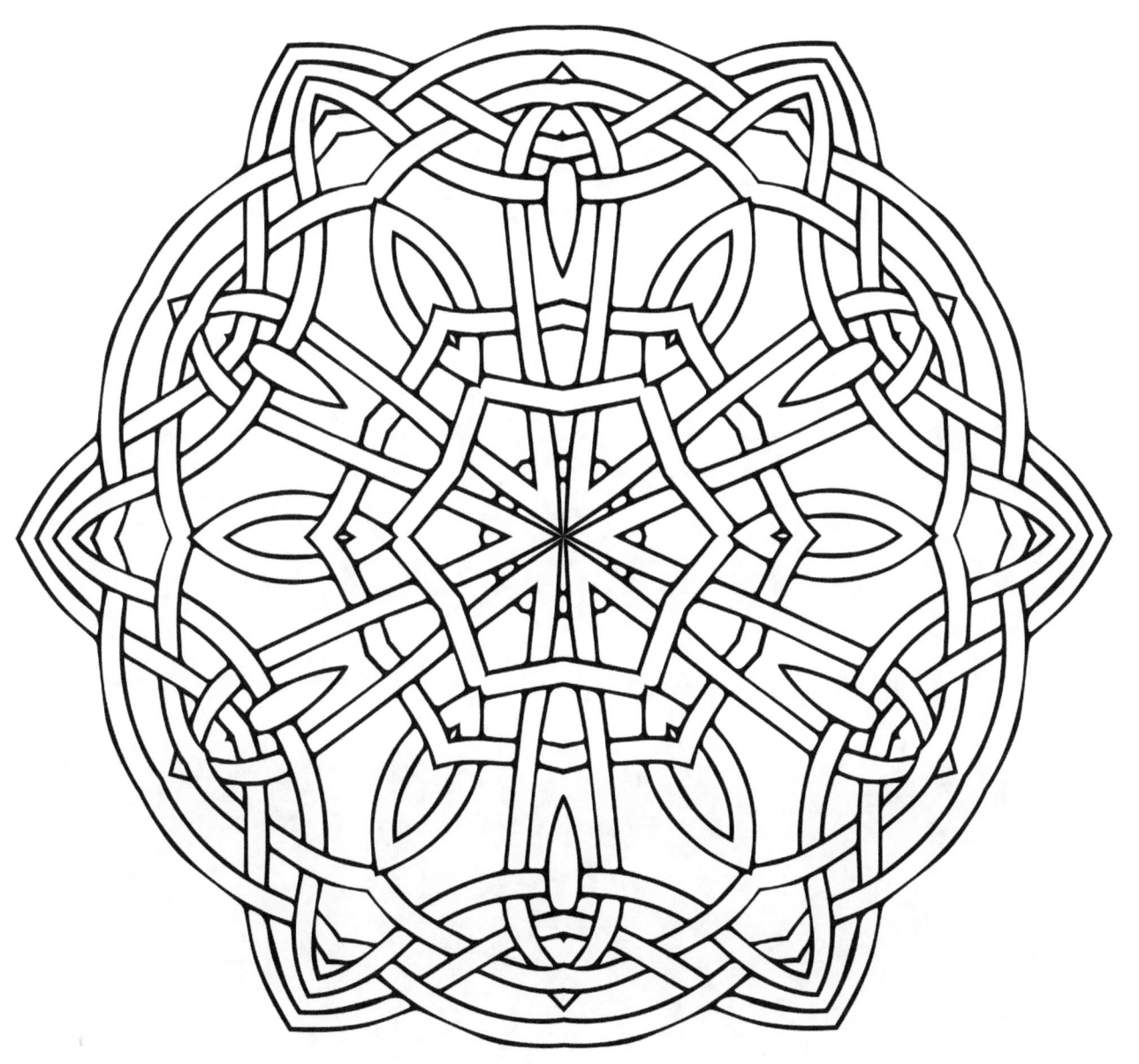

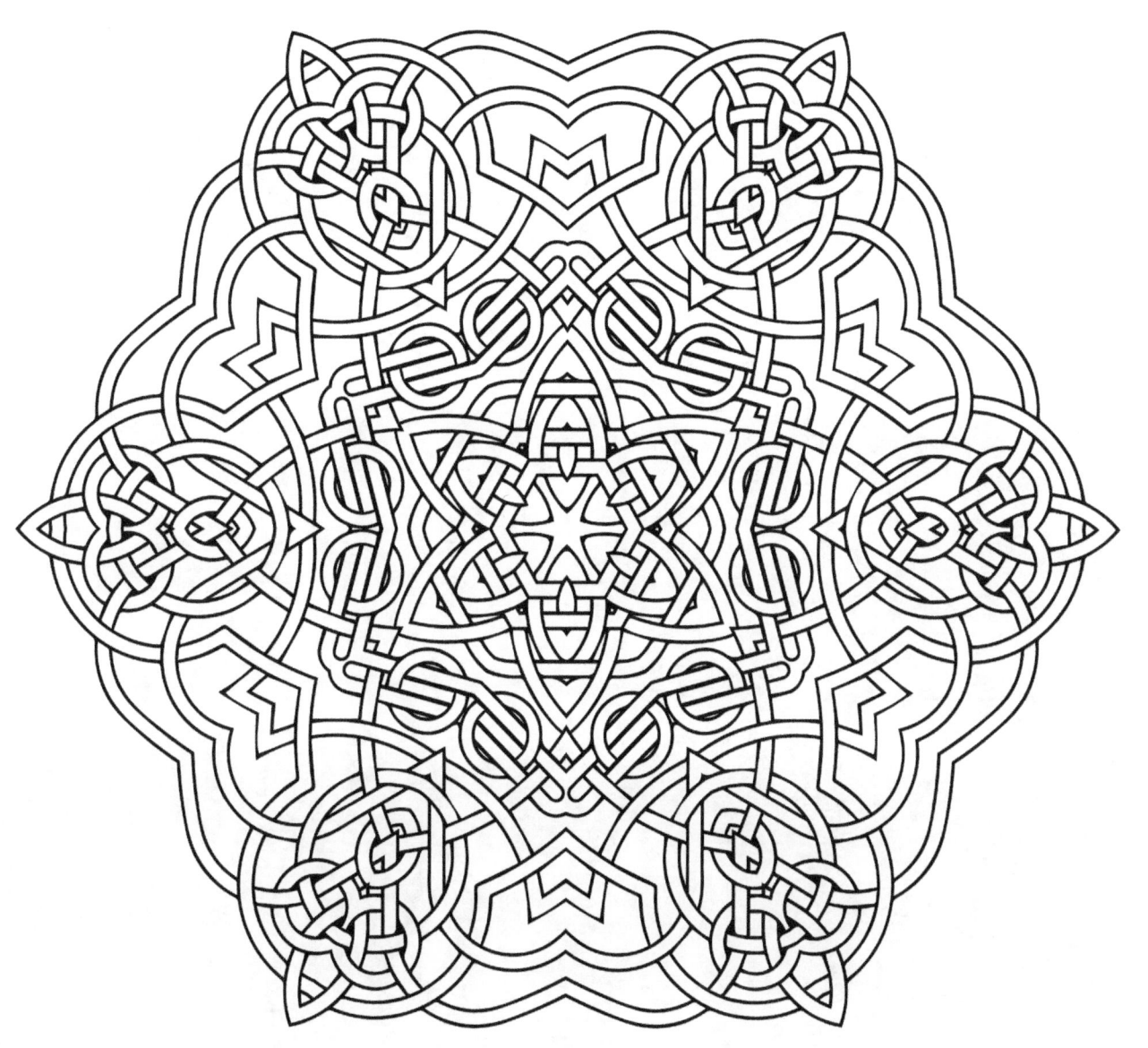

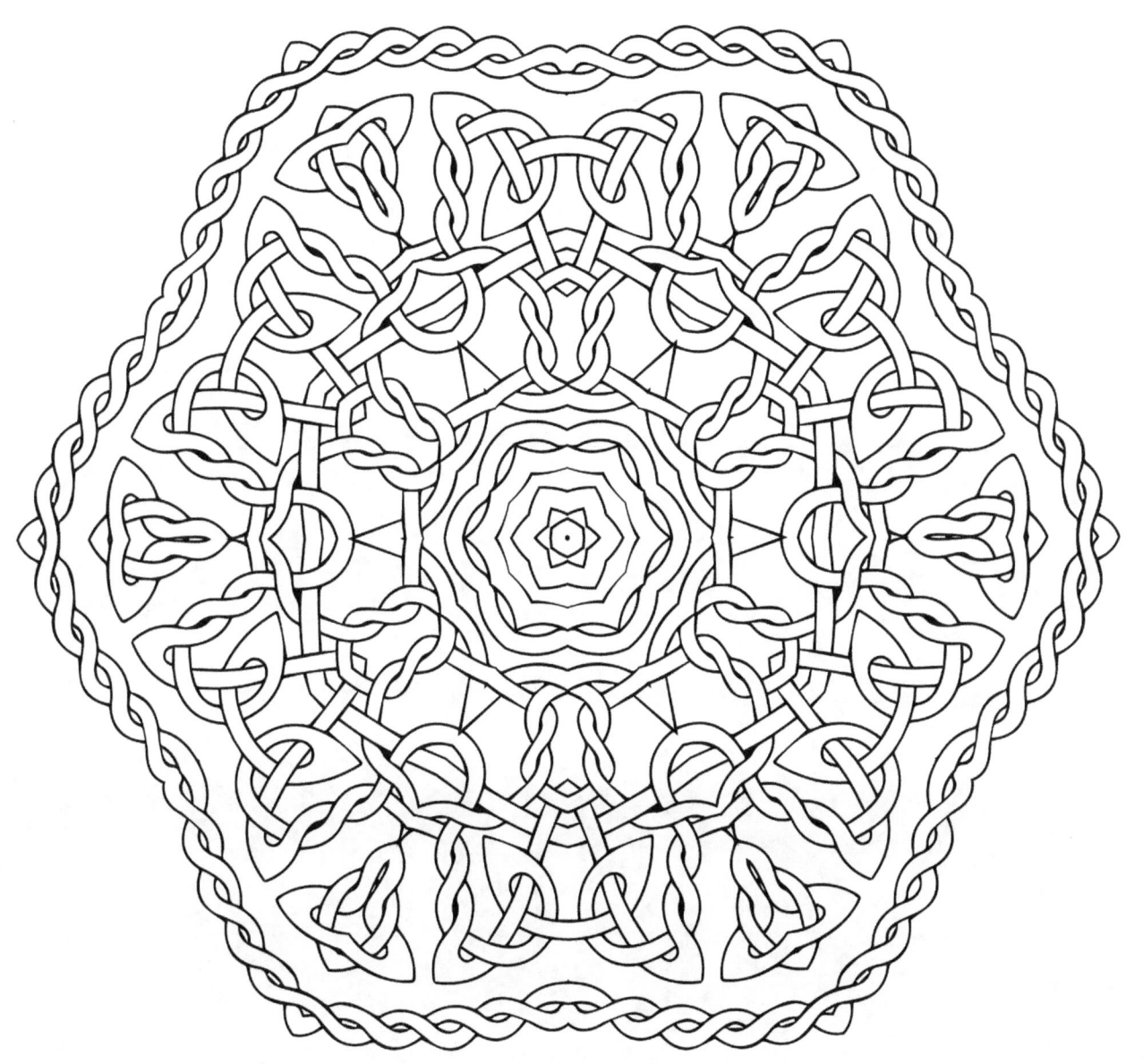

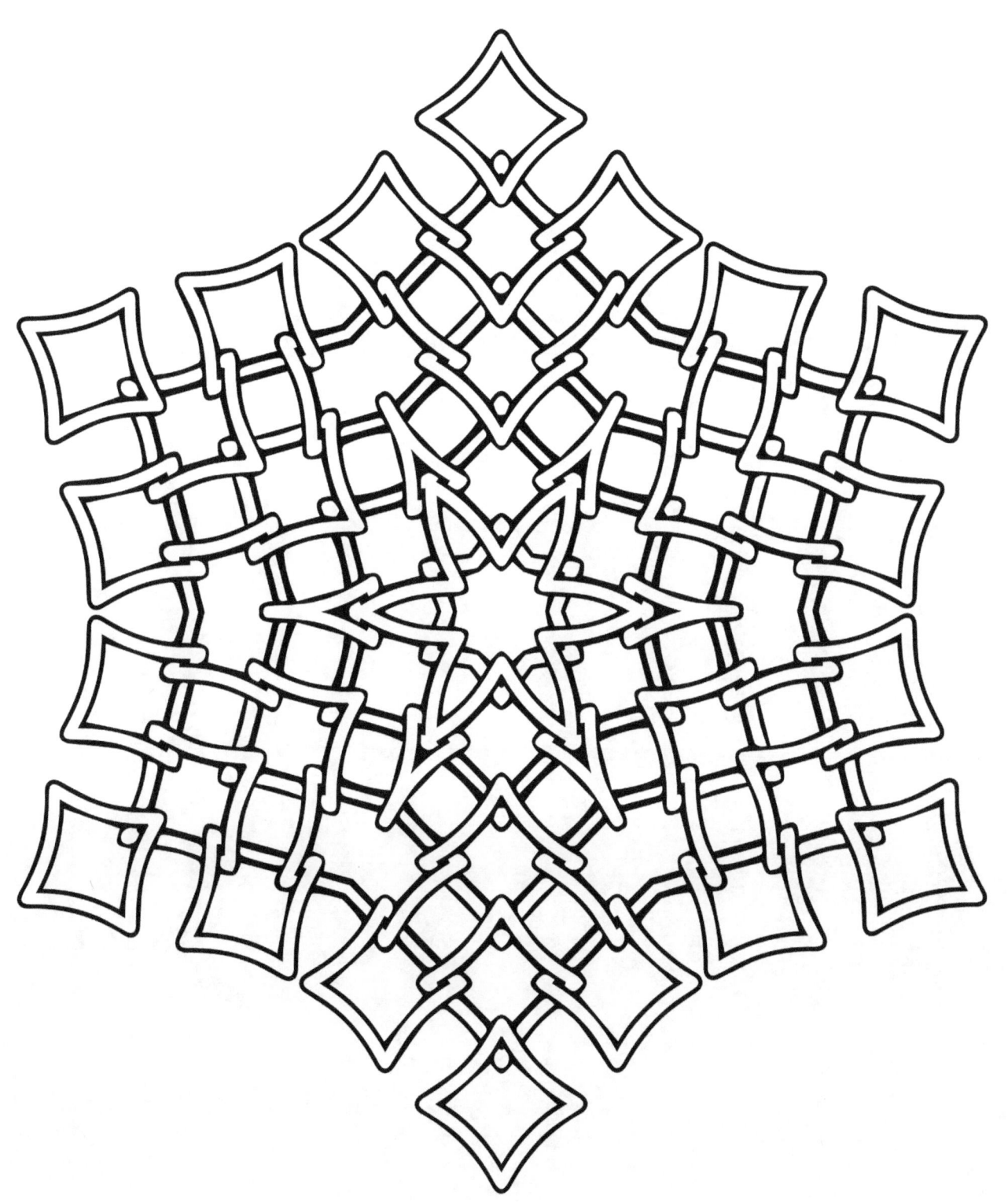

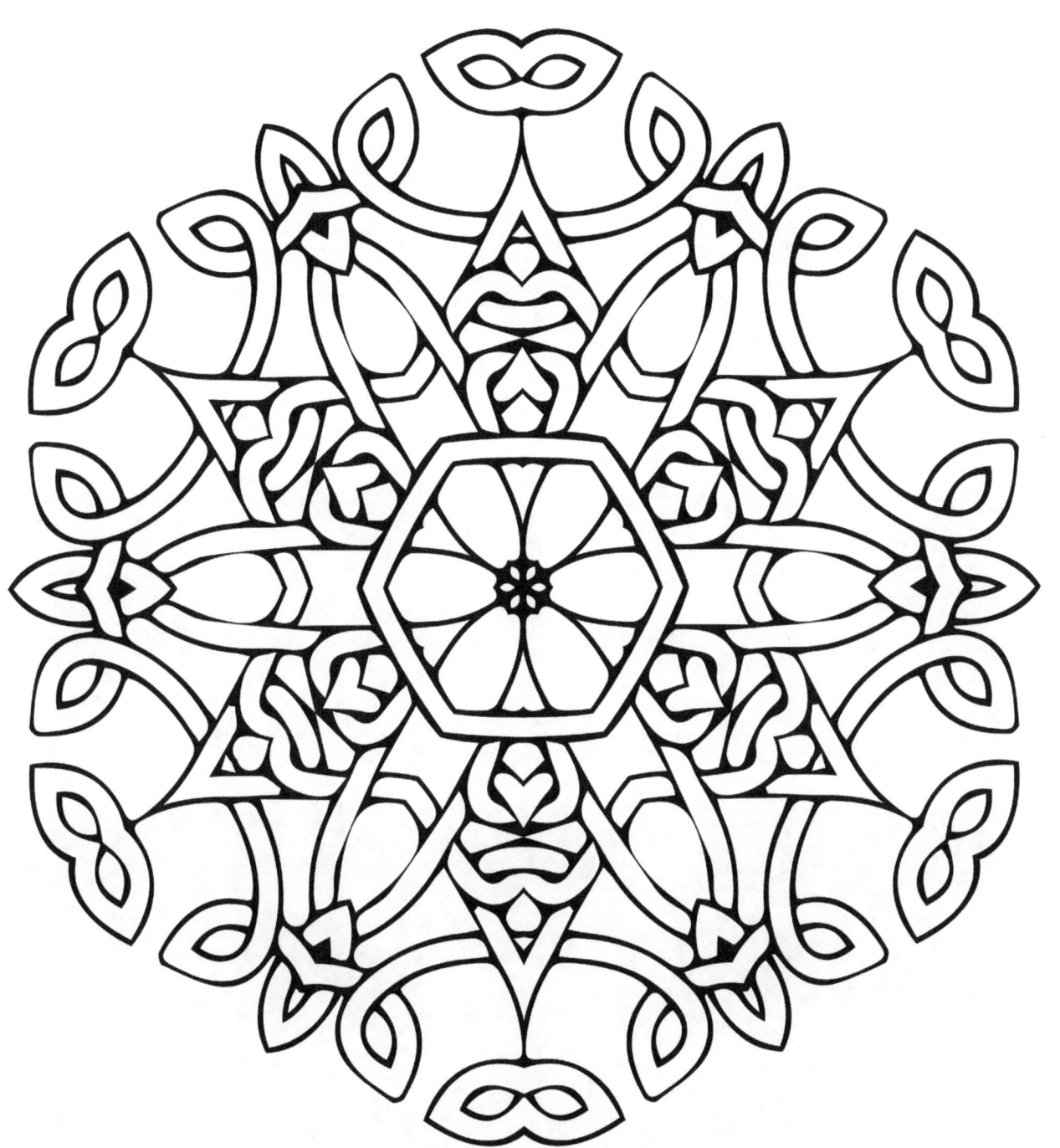

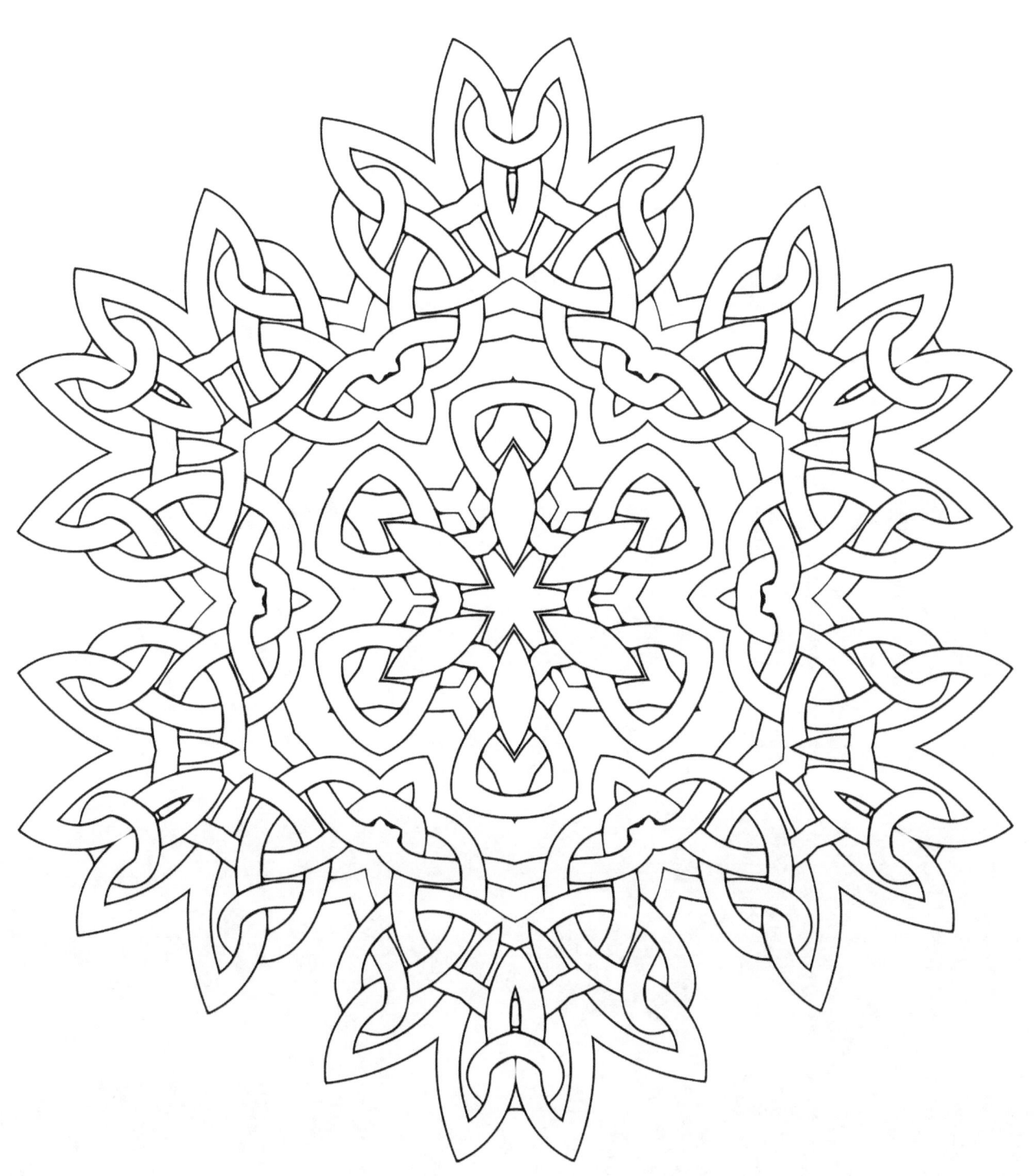

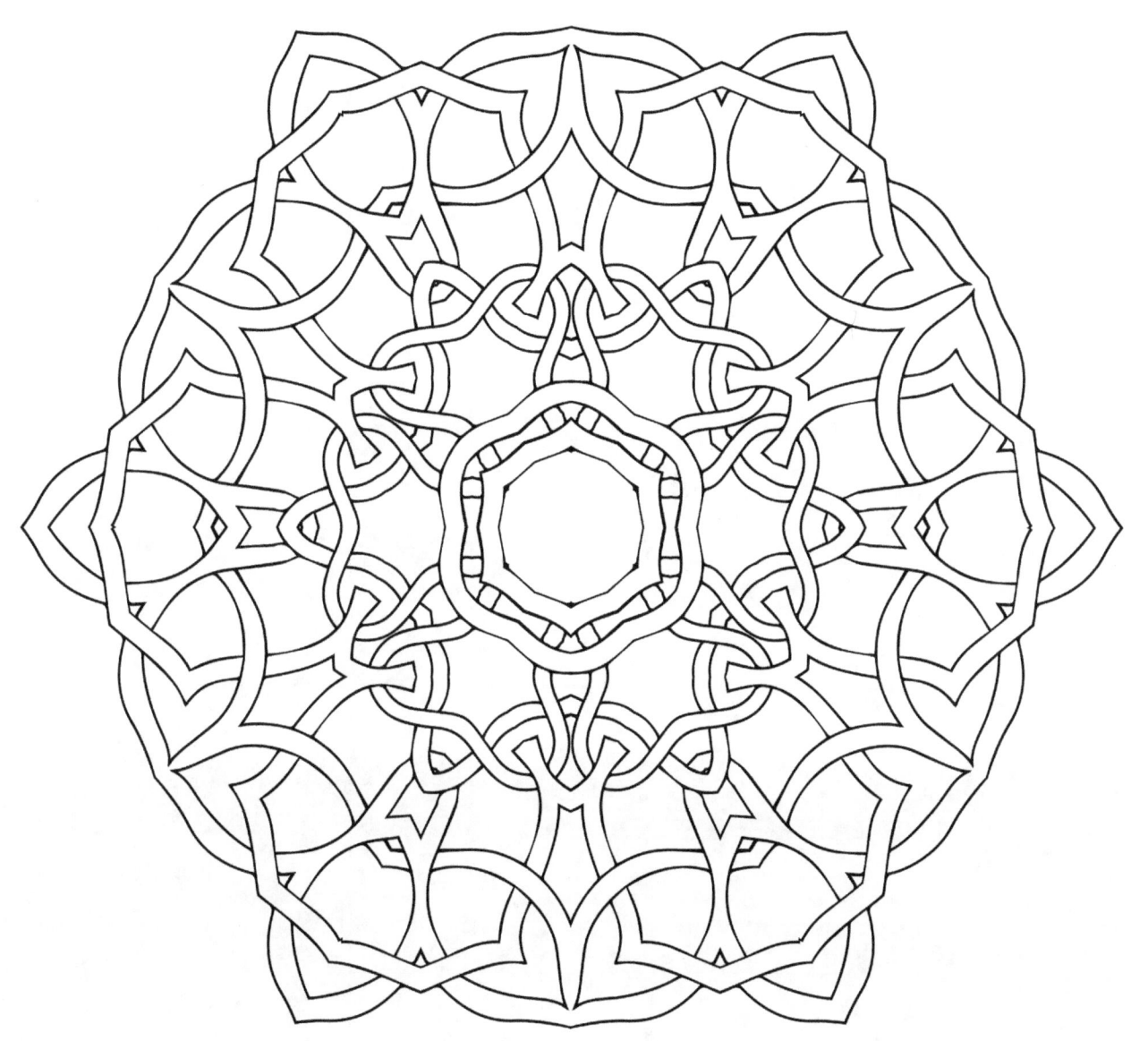

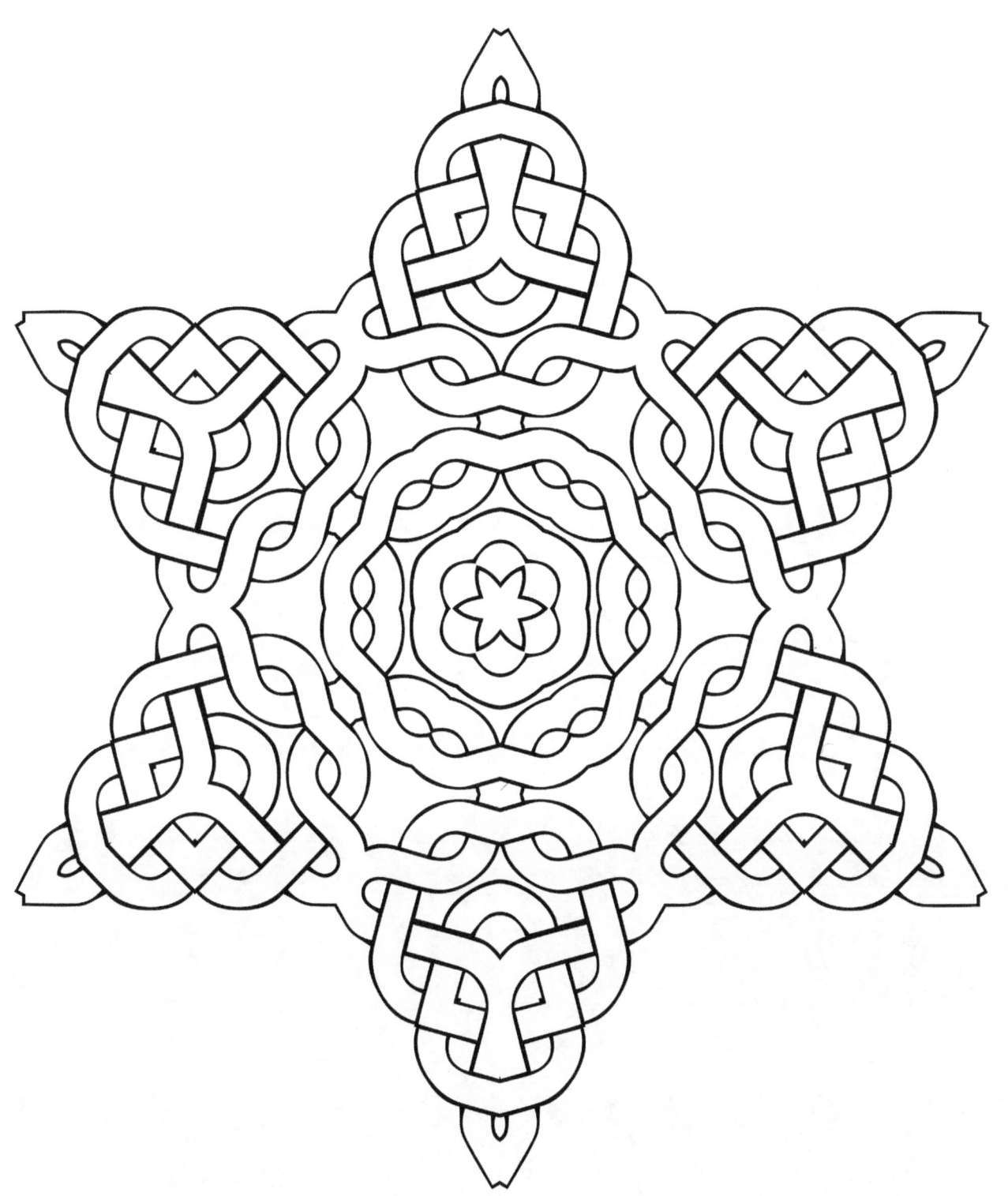

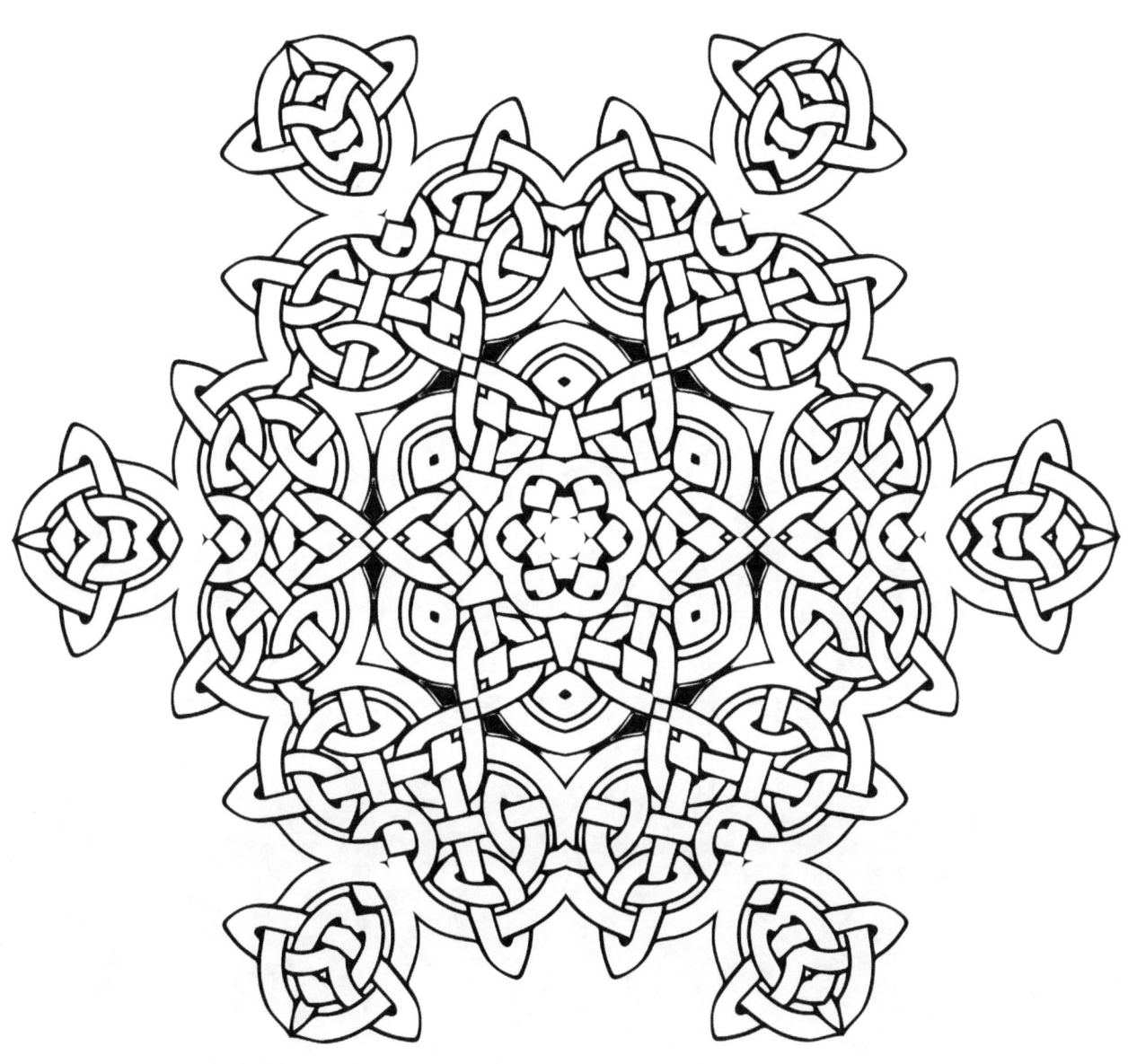

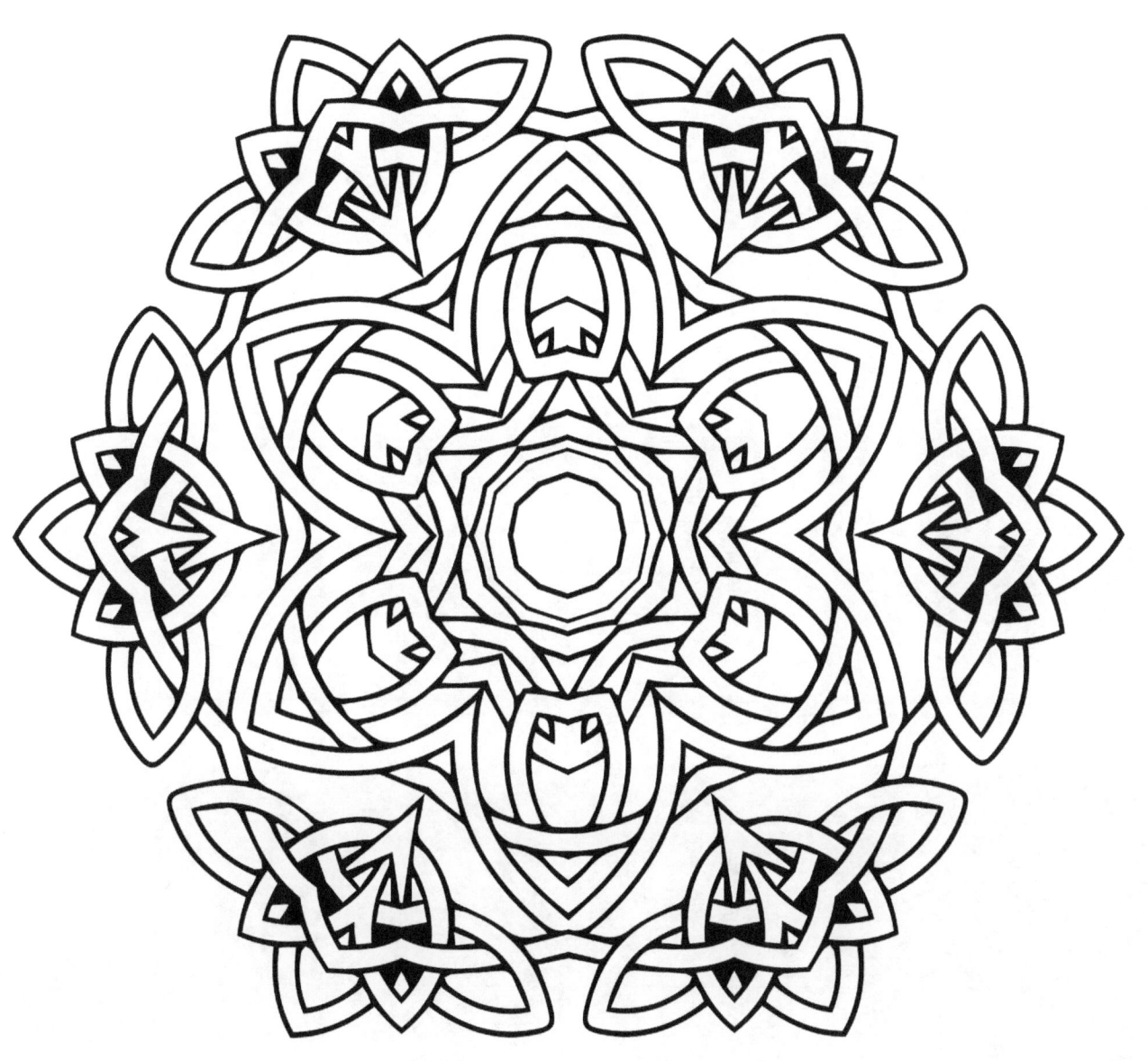

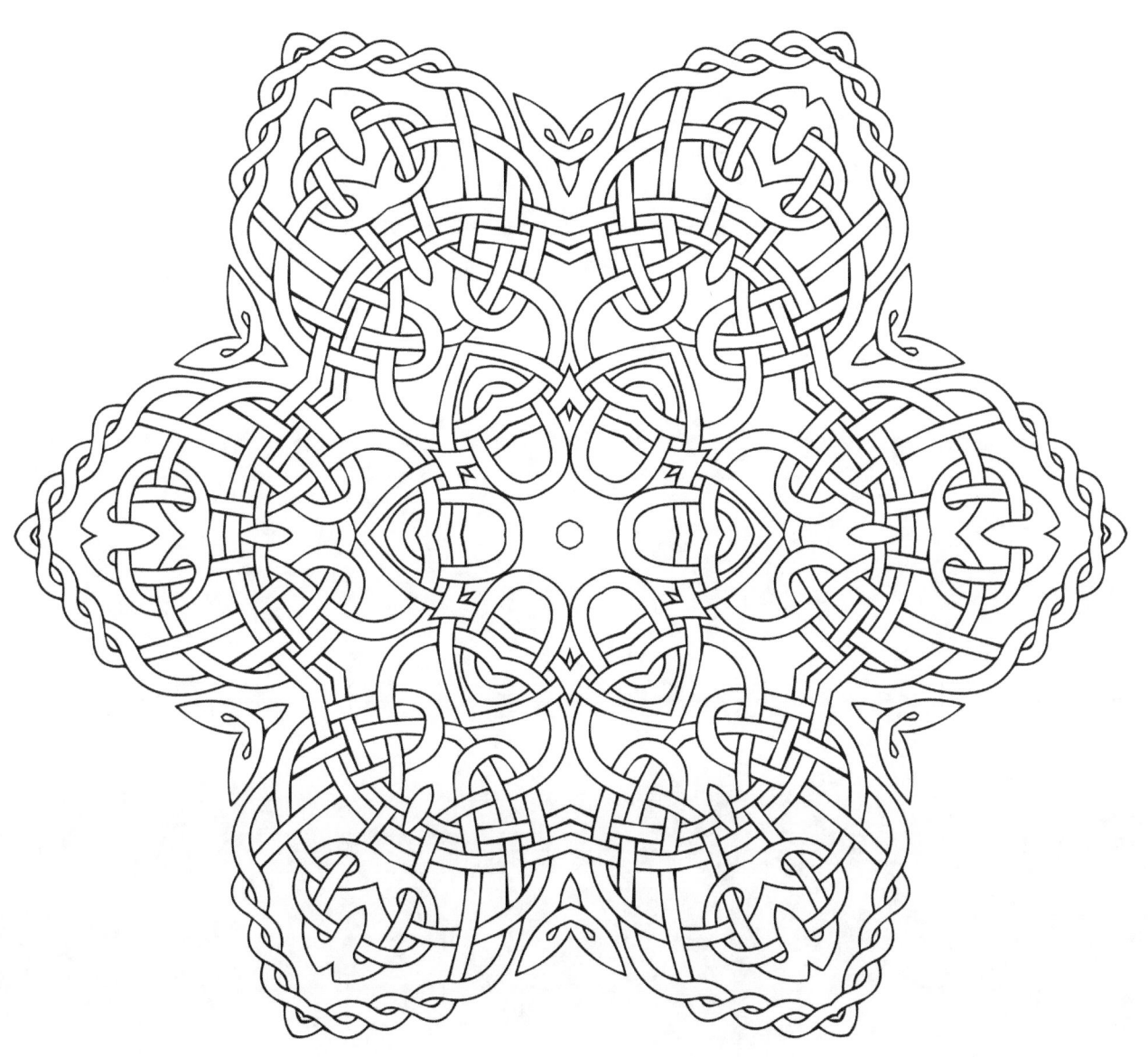

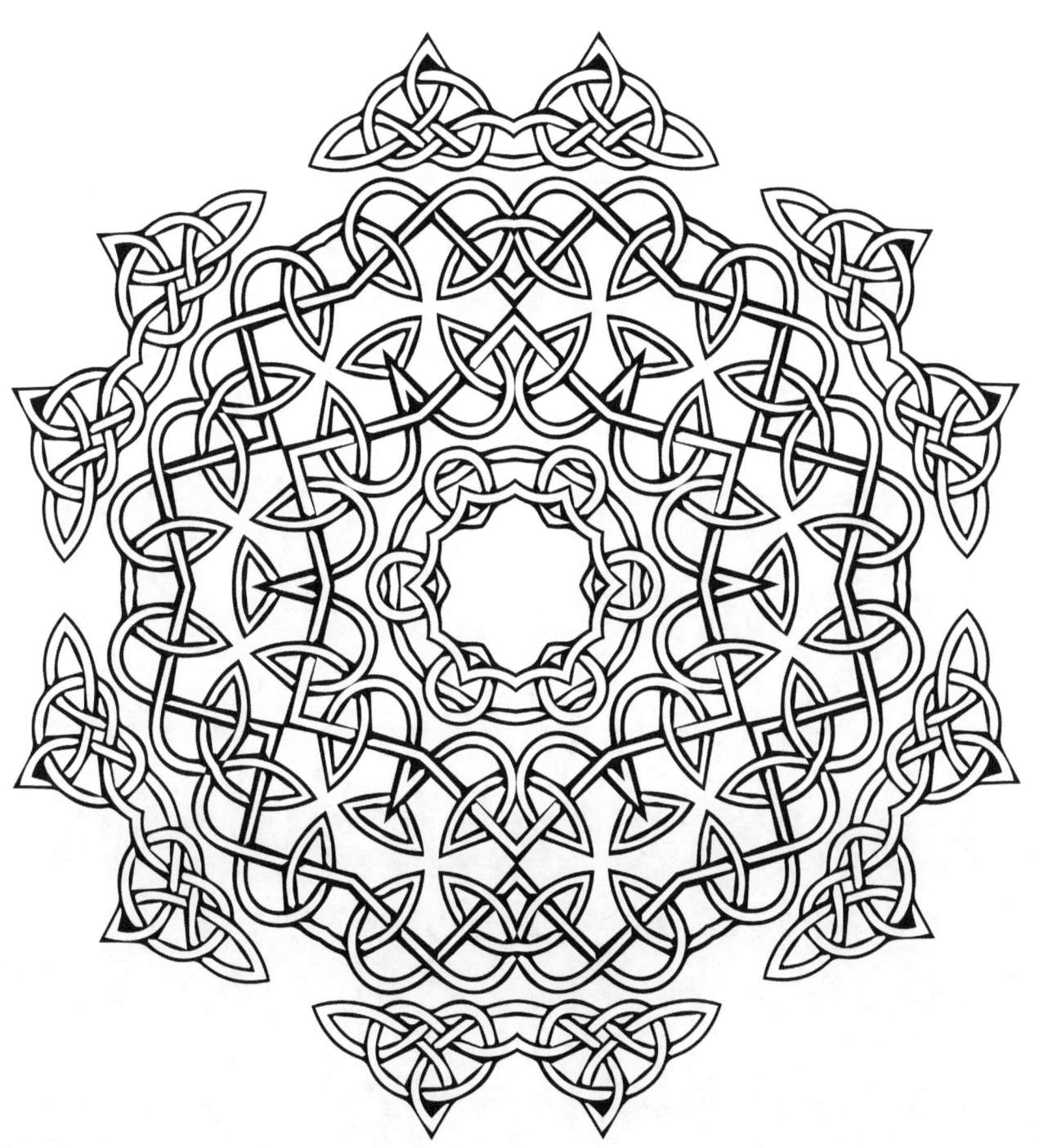

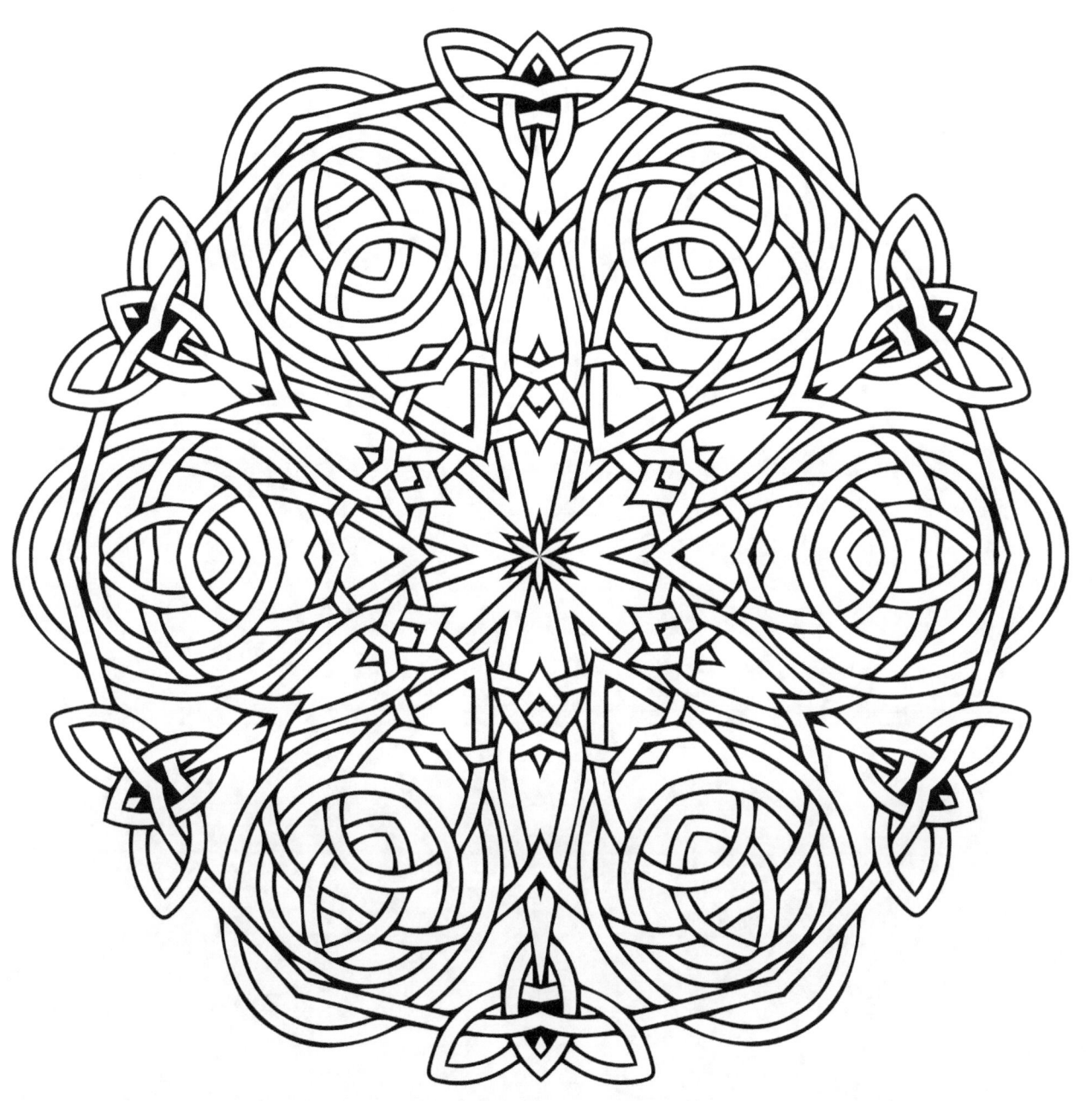

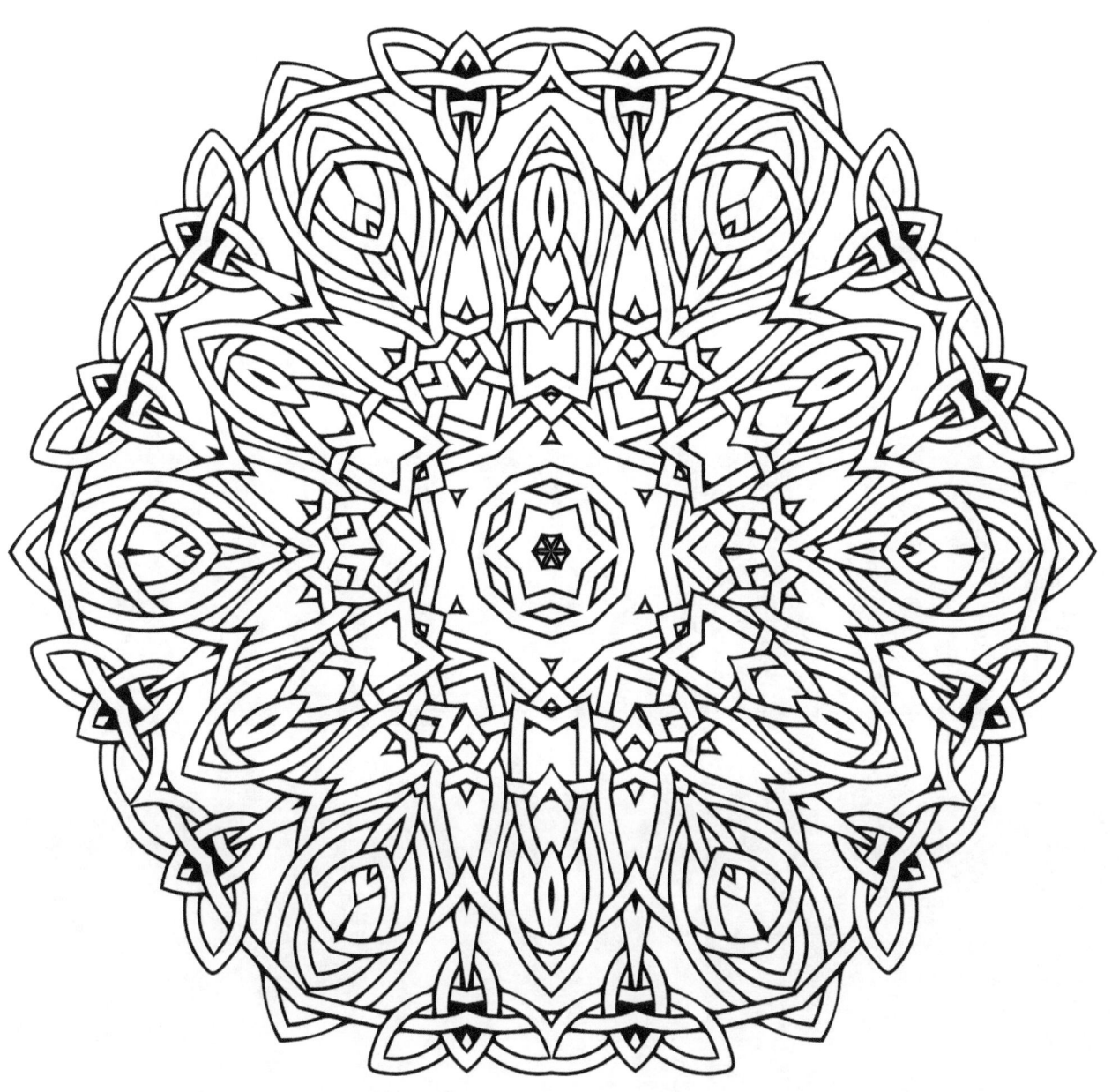

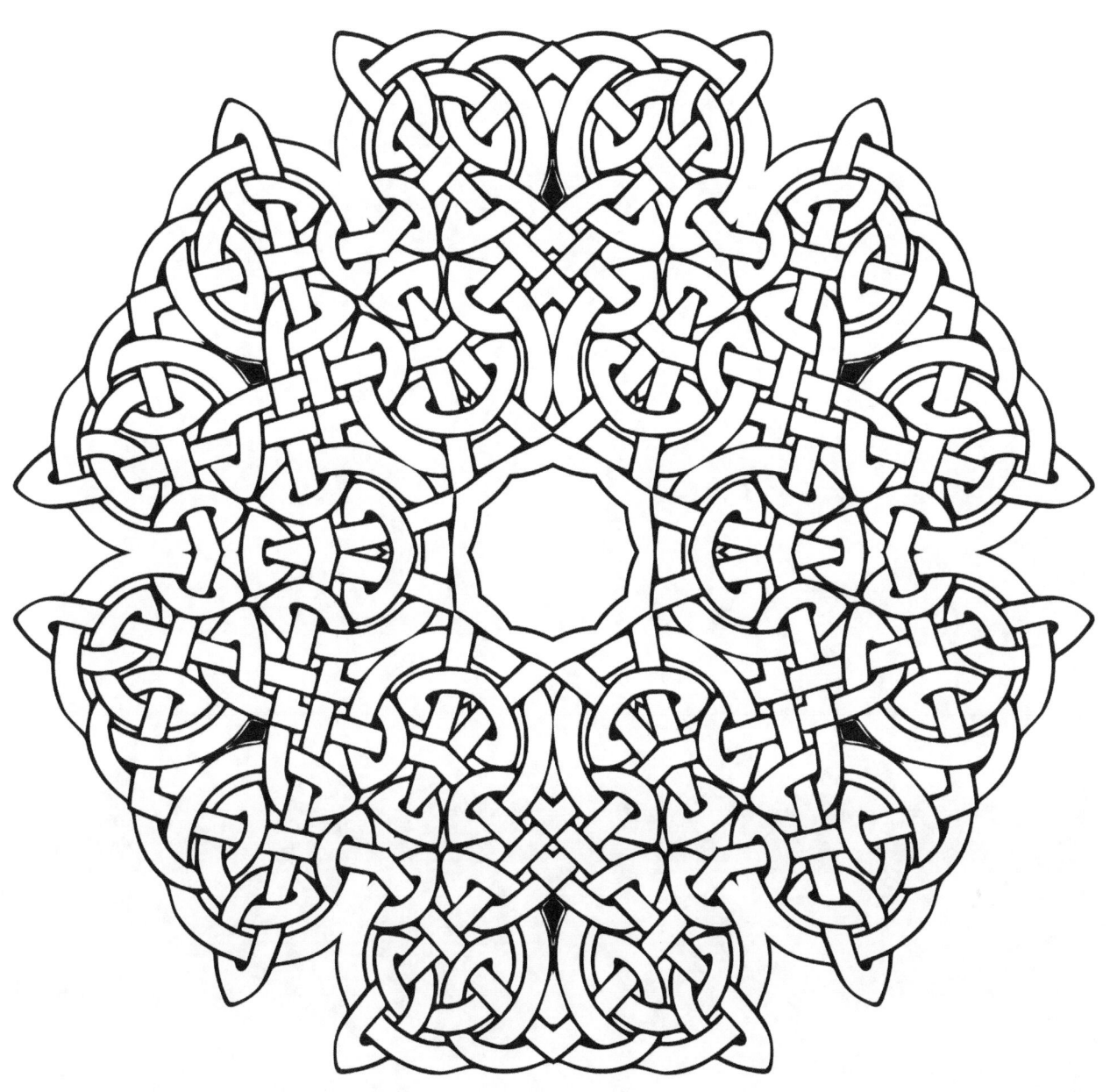

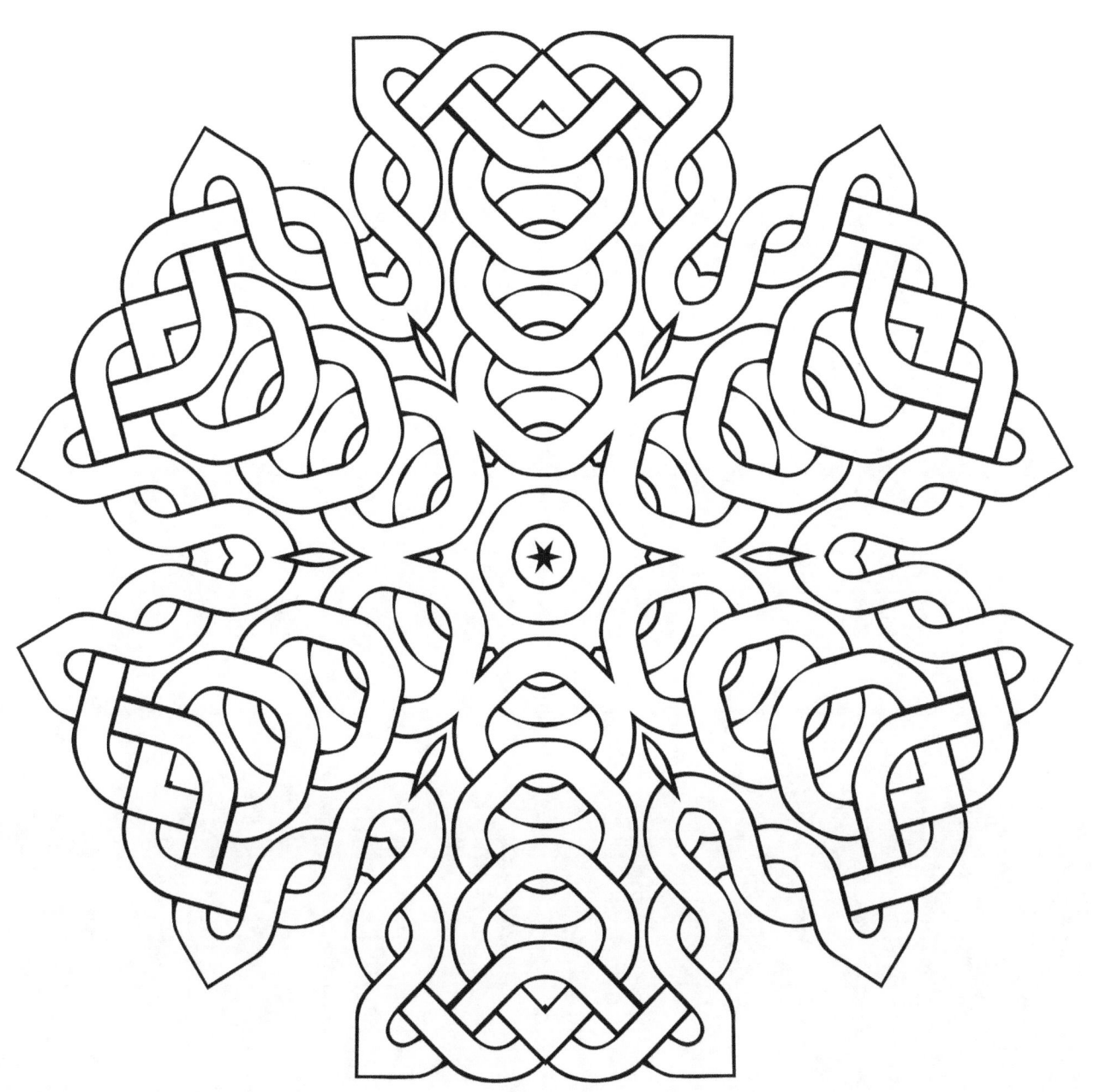

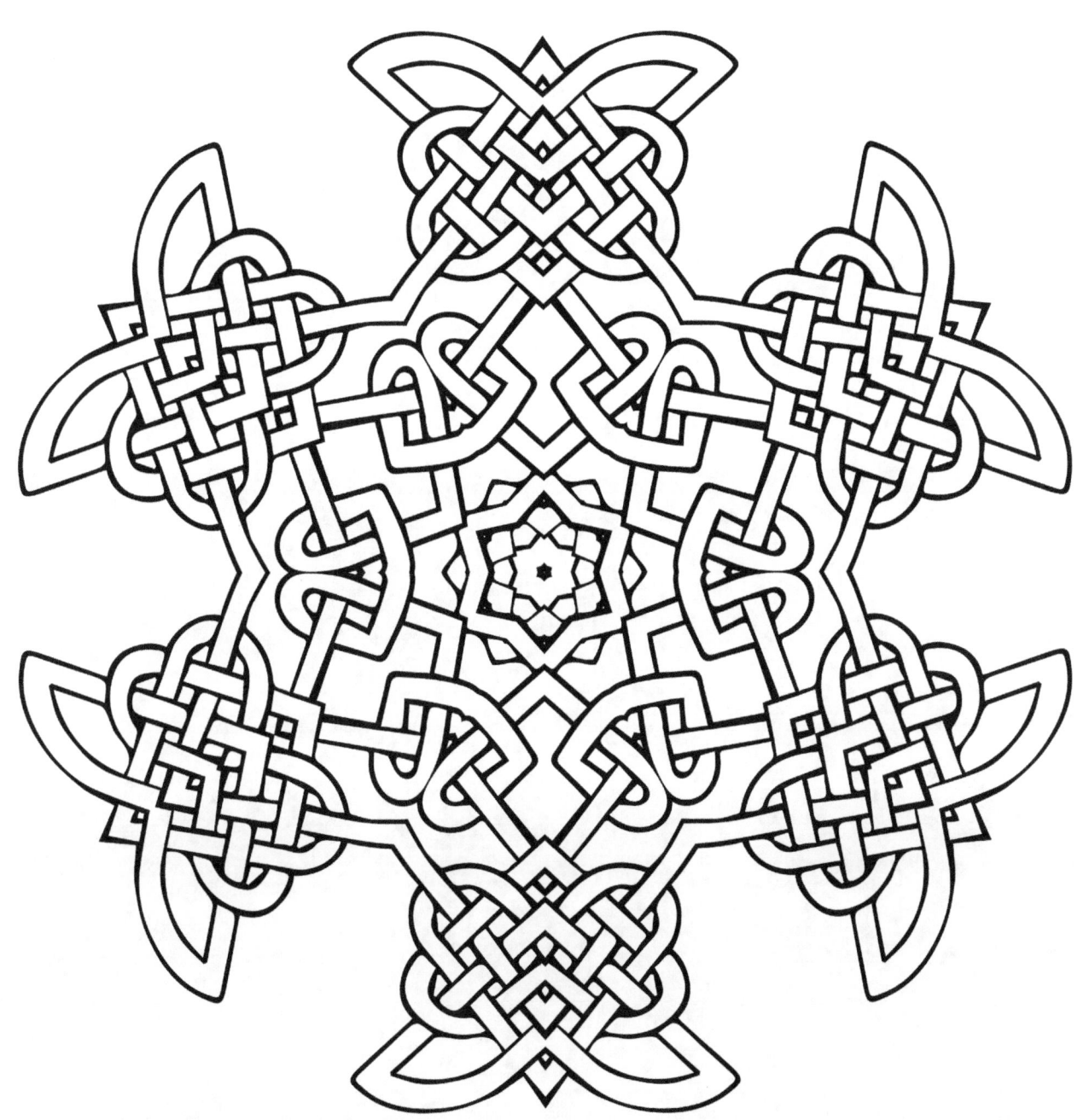

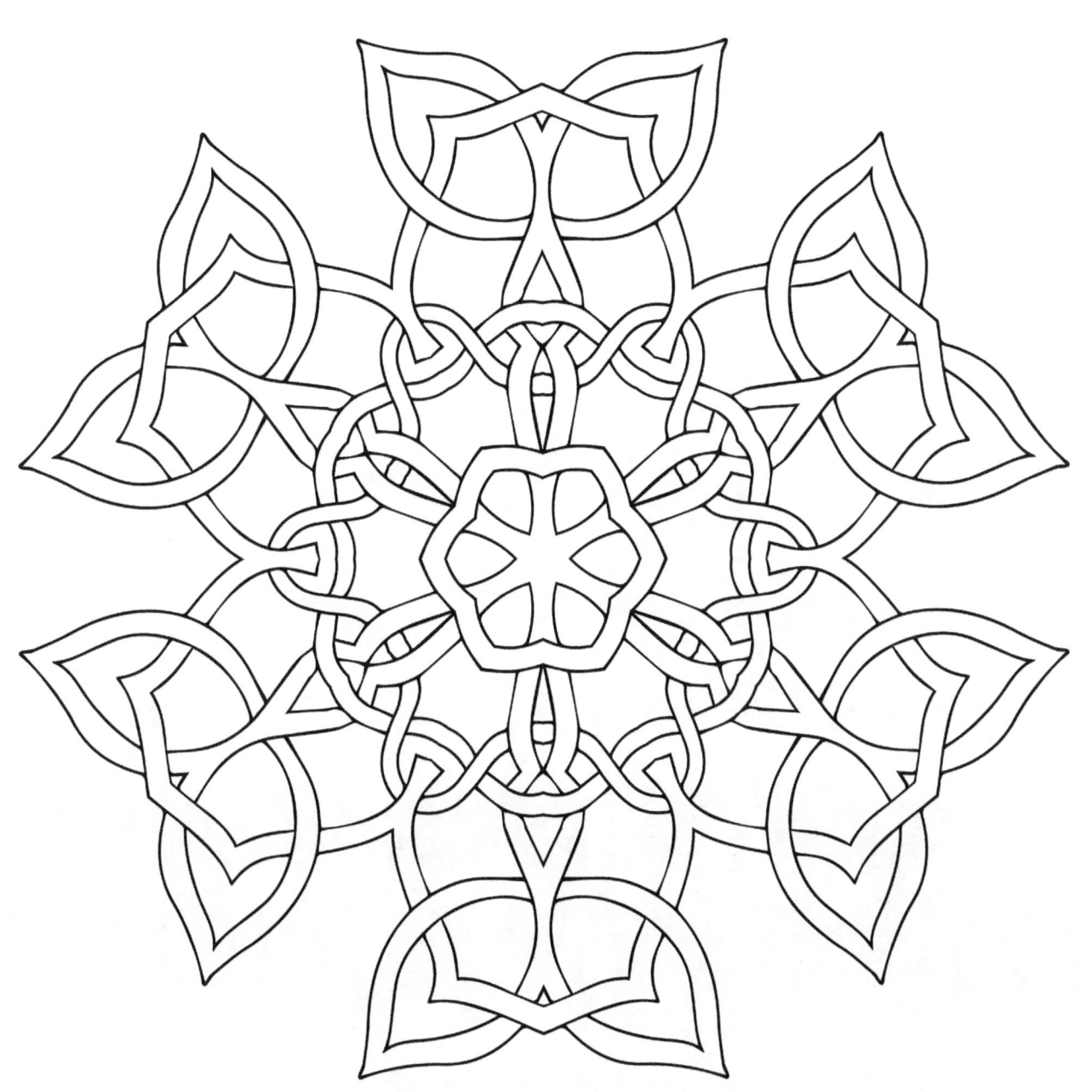

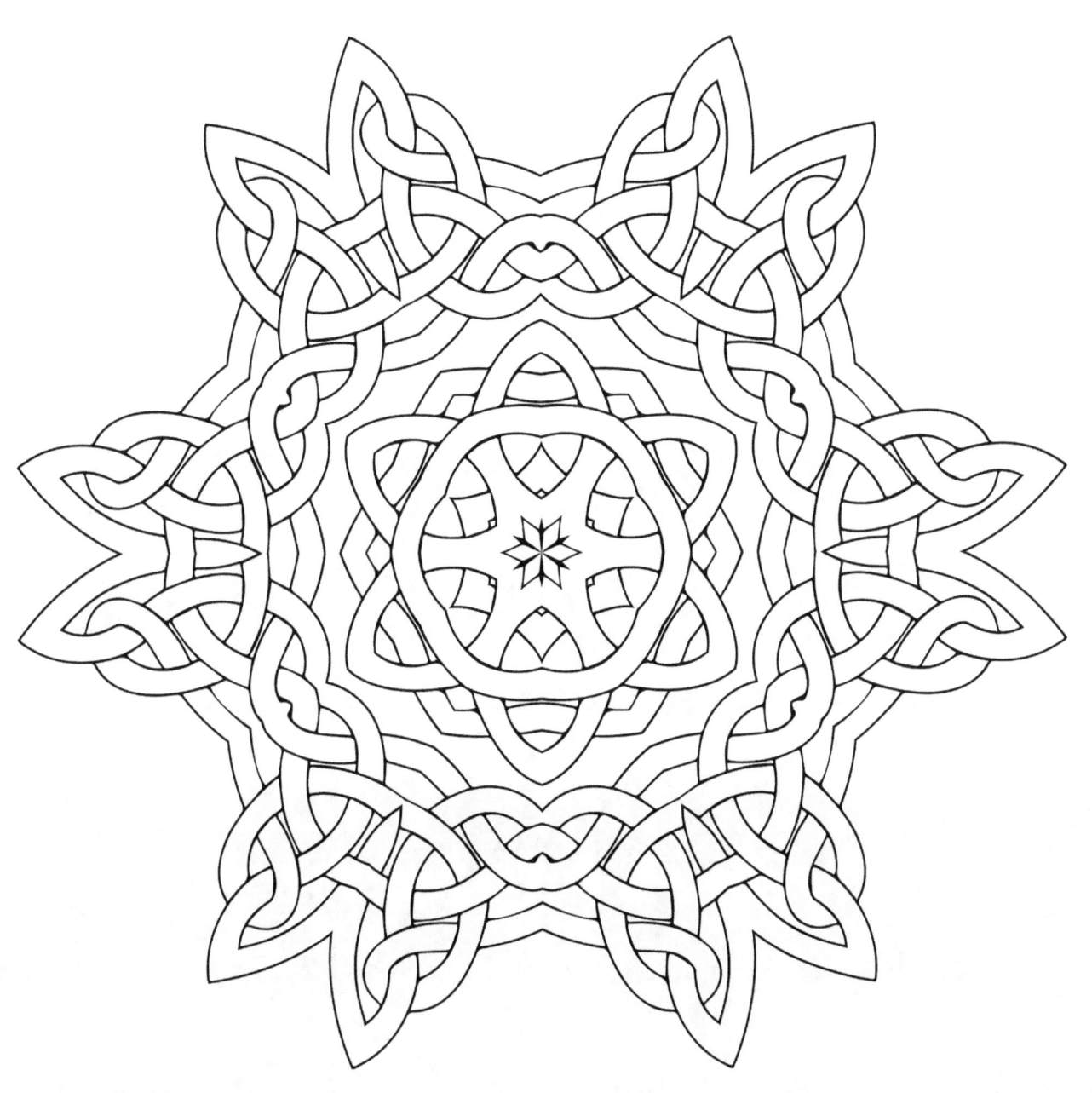

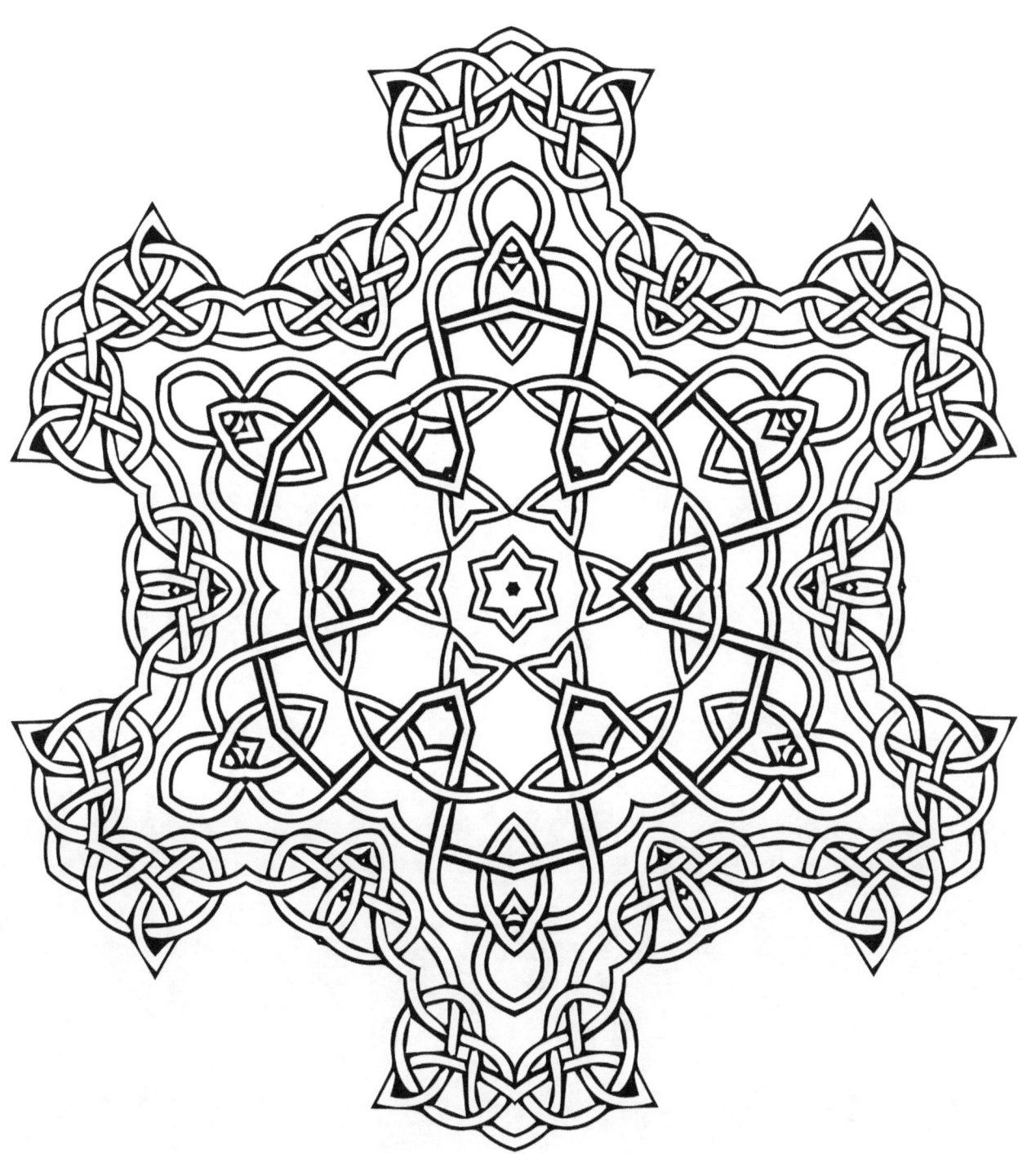

www.ingramcontent.com/pod-product-compliance
Lightning Source LLC
Chambersburg PA
CBHW080617180526
45168CB00007B/2944